My Appaloosa

A Journal for Anyone Interested in
Understanding Horses with bonus
insert on painting and drawing horses

by

Patricia J. Pasda, B.F.A, M.F.A.

Bloomington, IN   Milton Keynes, UK

AuthorHouse™
1663 Liberty Drive, Suite 200
Bloomington, IN 47403
www.authorhouse.com
Phone: 1-800-839-8640

AuthorHouse™ UK Ltd.
500 Avebury Boulevard
Central Milton Keynes, MK9 2BE
www.authorhouse.co.uk
Phone: 08001974150

First published by AuthorHouse 4/24/2007

ISBN: 978-1-4343-0871-9 (sc)

*Printed in the United States of America
Bloomington, Indiana*

This book is printed on acid-free paper.

My Appaloosa

A Journal for Anyone Interested in Understanding Horses with bonus insert on painting and drawing horses

By Patricia J. Pasda B.F.A. M.F.A.

Contents

Foreward xiii

Chapter One 1

Chapter Two 3

Chapter Three 41

Afterward 43

For Maryann, Joe, Mom, Dad, J, Gayle, Stacey, Nikki, Bev and Julie, Chester, Carrie, Ed, Katya, Nikki, Casey, Pam and all the horses in my herd

And for the Appaloosa

"The Lord is my shepherd, I shall not want.
He maketh me to lie down in green pastures;
He leadeth me beside the still waters."

Psalm 23

Foreward

Appaloosa heritage touches each of us in unique ways. Here, in America the wind blows where it wishes, and every corner of our land carries the whisper of the Appaloosa Horse. The Nez Perce Indians of the Northwest bred a loyal, sensitive, intelligent hard working horse unique in its striped hooves, whites of its eyes and many colors including spotted coats. Spanish ancestry, Nez Perce devotion to breeding and the Appaloosa Horse Club along with hundreds of devoted horseman help preserve the breed today. Present in all aspects of equestrian sports, Appaloosas continue to flourish in America. Every breeze you feel carries the Freedom of America and the call of the Appaloosa horses who call her home, past and present.

I am an artist, in every aspect of my life.

The way I dress, how I think, how I live, how I paint and write, and yes, I am an artist in how I approach horses.

I use the creative process. That elusive creativity that gives projects energy .

In these pages I describe how the creative process can work in developing a relationship with a horse.

Things to keep in mind include how you breathe and how you approach a horse.

Chapter One
Breathe

Introductions to a horse are simple. A horse takes you in, breathing deeply to catch your aura and way of being. They remember you forever, and know where you have been, where you are and what kind of heart you have.

They remember how you treat them always.

Echoes

Horses echo what is in our minds and hearts. They know us instantly and what baggage we carry to the barn affects our time there. When we are afraid, they are afraid.

When we are sure, they are sure.

Horses have large hearts and strong spirits. They echo back to us who we really are at any given moment.

Horse Owners as Friends...

My friendship with Gayle of Hopelock Farm opened my heart and mind to the spirit of the Appaloosa.

I also have another friend who trains and breeds appaloosas, Nikki. The friendships you develop and resulting trust and training at any stable contributes to your comfort, safety and level of horsemanship. Know the atmosphere, purpose and type of training available at all the stables in your region before you choose one as home.

Chapter Two
The Quest for an Equestrian Life

I remember one summer day when I was thirteen years old. It was the perfect day.

I was on a horse farm in Buck County. I had ridden Rosie, cleaned stalls, watered and fed horses, taken horses to and from pastures, saddled school horses and tended to sick ones since four am that morning.

Now, at 7 pm I was totally content. Rosie grazed beside me, and whinnied a "Here I am" to her stablemates.

Years later, upon the illness of my Father, I needed to find myself again.

I held the photo of me from that day and eyed the self confident girl in the photo.

I knew what I had to do. Step by step, here is a guide, a step by step plan for anyone, old or young who wants to learn how to become a friend, rider, caretaker or owner of horses.

Step One

Research stables.

English

Western

Dressage

Breed

Some owners teach and some hire instructors.

Write your research here _____

_____

_____

_____

_____

_____

_____

_____

_____

_____

_____

_____

Phone numbers and addresses _____

_____

_____

_____

_____

_____

_____

_____

_____

_____

_____

_____

Local stables _____

_____

_____

_____

_____

_____

_____

_____

_____

_____

_____

Horse Organizations _____

_____

_____

_____

_____

_____

_____

_____

_____

_____

_____

_____

Horse Magazines _____

_____

_____

_____

_____

_____

_____

_____

_____

_____

Types of Barns in my area _____

_____

_____

_____

_____

_____

_____

_____

_____

_____

_____

Types of Riding in my area _____

_____

_____

_____

_____

_____

_____

_____

_____

_____

_____

_____

Instructors _____

_____

_____

_____

_____

_____

_____

_____

_____

_____

_____

_____

Horse books _____

_____

_____

_____

_____

_____

_____

_____

_____

_____

_____

Step Two

Research horse breeds. Many have organizations devoted to that particular breed.

Step Three

Horseback riding lessons.

What they are really like. _____

_____

_____

_____

_____

_____

_____

_____

_____

Saddles

Lessons often begin with learning how to put a saddle on a horse at that particular establishment. Listen closely and keep this journal in the following pages. Mark what height you need your stirrup to be placed, what horse uses what bit, how to hang a bridle on the wall or any other details that are required when you ride. _____

_____

_____

_____

_____

_____

_____

_____

Brushing a horse

Write instructions from your lesson here.

Curry _____

_____

_____

_____

_____

_____

_____

_____

_____

Dandy _____

_____

_____

_____

_____

_____

_____

_____

_____

_____

_____

_____

Finishing

Hoof Pick _____

_____

_____

_____

_____

_____

_____

_____

_____

_____

_____

_____

Bridle _____

_____

_____

_____

_____

_____

_____

_____

_____

_____

_____

_____

Halter _____

_____

_____

_____

_____

_____

_____

_____

_____

_____

_____

Helpful hints

Remember horses see in both directions and have several blind spots, directly in front of them, directly behind them and underneath them.

Sound matters. Always let a horse know when you are approaching them.

While many instructors focus on riding, ask to learn ground work, and longeing. Write your notes here. _____

_____

_____

_____

_____

_____

_____

Touching horses

Approach a horse slowly, eyes down. Pet them on the neck and forehead slowly and let them know you are comfortable with them.

Take time.

Never let them feel you are rushed even if time is short.

If you are angry of upset wait to go to the stable until you are calm and collected.

Thunder can bring out the instinct to run.

The wind is very scary… to any horse.

Clothing for the rider

Proper attire is very important for the type of riding you are learning. Listen to your instructor and never wear loose fitting clothing and always wear boots. Gloves are helpful in any discipline.

Every stable trains their horses for a particular discipline and temperament...write the type of clothing you will need below.

_____

_____

_____

_____

_____

_____

_____

_____

_____

_____

Muddy Pastures

Spring and Fall bring muddy, slippery conditions to pastures and walkways. Wear non- slip water-proof boots .

You can bring your riding boots to the barn separately and keep them just for riding, and not for walking in the mud.

Fear

If a horse senses that a person nearby is afraid they know that person is telling them to be afraid, but they are not sure what to be afraid of… they have no idea the person is afraid of them, they only sense that fear is present.

Listen

Learn to listen, and to watch. A muscle flinching, an ear in a certain position, or a change in eye expression can tell you everything about what a horse is about to do.

The eye is the gateway to the mood in a particular moment in a horse's life. Listen and watch and understand what you see, study horse behavior books and sit and watch horses.

Observations _____

_____

_____

_____

_____

_____

_____

_____

_____

Terms to research

Mane

Bridle

Lead rope

Halter

Saddle

Saddle pad

Boots

Breeches

Gloves

Helmet

Fetlock

Turn on the haunches

Right lead

Left lead

Barn

Stall

Cross ties

Withers

Curry

Dandy

Finishing brush

Whoa

Trot

Canter

Jog

Lope

Arena

Stall

Hay

Feed

Sweet feed

Pellets

Walk

Pasture

Ring

Hands

Write terms you need to learn more about here _____

_____

_____

_____

_____

_____

Horse Stories

The best way I know to help anyone understand horses is to tell stories of experiences I have had with these grand creatures. Since I am an artist I use the creative process to understand my horse friends.

The Clydesdale

The first time I saw him, the Clydesdale was running across the pasture, screeching and bucking, challenging anyone to come near him. Thin and overworked, the large 2400 pound horse paced and shook his head, eyes flashing and mane and tail flying in the wind.

I sat outside the big white fence for hours studying him and waited until the sun began to set on a warm spring evening. I waited, and watched.

About 8 pm he walked to the fence. He stood in front of me, eyeing me. Quiet and still. The big blue eyes glistened with a friendly glow, his ears forward, he gently bent and leaned over the fence to take the bit of apple I held out of my left hand.

I sat still.

He leaned forward and down, offering his great broad forehead for me to pet. I reached out and stroked his magnificent head, and we both sat , quietly watching the night sky.

He slept. I dreamed.

Over the next few months I fed him carrots and apples every day. I walked beside him and taught him to walk with a halter on his head, and a lead rope attached to the halter. His hair grew back, his thin frame filled in, he became healthy and beautiful once again, the big bay Clydesdale with the white socks.

The Older Horse

Wisdom of time teaches older horses how to read people easily and quickly. They know you instantly and often express emotion through how you feel. The older horse sees how you see, knows about your past and present and everything about you in an instant. They need care, compassion, special medications and foods.

Head out of His Stall, Guardian of the Herd

Every morning when I arrived the huge horse held his head high out of his stall door and eyed me. He checked every arrival at the barn. Under clear skies, stormy skies, at dusk and dawn, the leader of the herd remained ever vigilant, strong sentinel protecting his horses and his people.

Lift Up Your Hoof

Sometimes all it takes is humor and patience in addition to strong leadership to get a horse to listen.

I was attempting to treat a weak hoof of one horse and he refused to lift it for me no matter how I signaled him or asked. Rather that scold him I stood up and looked at him with a smile…"Ok, if you keep your hoof down for everyone who tries to lift it, no wonder it needs medication." I commented looking him gently in the eye. "If you would lift it up for me I could treat it and clean it and you will feel better." He looked at me a moment and calmly lifted his hoof.

Morning Sun

I arrived at the farm early one morning, parked and got out of my car. Across the entrance to the arena, in a far off pasture stood a strawberry roan Appaloosa, his Coat glistening in the morning sun. Bright against the blue sky and green pasture, you could feel the appaloosas of the past and present, visualized in the beauty of the moment.

Longeing in the Morning

I took the spotted grey appaloosa mare out to the stall, and prepared for morning exercise. In usual manner, she glared at me and pretended not to want anything.

I rubbed her neck and she responded with soft eyes. In the ring on the lunge line, she bucked and ran and galloped in circles around me over the blue snow.

The Truck

The tractor trailer arrived at the farm to deliver hay on schedule, his schedule. What he didn't realize was that the horse on the cross ties didn't like trucks.

He pulled into the driveway and air brakes sounded loudly. The blue roan Appaloosa mare's eyes grew wide in fear as she struggled for freedom. I loosened the clips and calmed her with my voice and led her behind the barn to a pasture, the truck and sounds left behind.

The Leaf Blower

We walked across the grass, the horse and I, enjoying the fall air and the blue sky overhead.

A gardener across the pasture turned on a leaf blower to clear a driveway. The horse took fright, his eyes grew wide and he reared up in fear. Then he remembered I was on the other end of the lead rope. He calmed a moment, stood still and eyed me. His look said, I am really afraid and it is a good idea to move away from that strange loud object over there. I led him back to his stall, the beautiful horse who calmed and stayed with me despite his fear.

Write your own stories in the following pages. My stories serve as examples. _____

_____

_____

_____

_____

_____

_____

_____

_____

_____

Chapter Three
B.

Racehorse, hunter, western pleasure, lesson horse, great big quarter horse appendix with a big heart, He could do it all and did.

He could move hearts, and mend hearts.

Reliable B, companion forever to so many, He taught me about who I am than I ever thought possible.

Thank you B.

Take the time so spend with any horse you ride. Walking, brushing, grazing…you will get more back than you can possibly imagine.

Afterward
A Horses Voice

I love it here in my stall, a twelve by twelve foot space just for me. Cedar chips are soft under my hooves. In the front right corner I have a feed bin where I eat grains and treats. To my left I have lots of hay so I can munch when I am not outside in the pasture. My herd has nine horse members, and several human members. Most of the horses are bigger than I am.

In the winter I wear a coat to keep me warm and I always have shoes on my feet.

Sometimes I eat carrots and apples. I am cute and loving so I get lots of attention.

If you think about it, a horse sees you as the one who knows what to do, who will let him know what is expected of him.

So make sure you study and learn and know how to walk a horse, brush a horse, and approach a horse before you ride one.

They trust and look up to us. The study of horses can help us understand ourselves better, and help us heal. For more information on the Appaloosa, write to the Appaloosa Horse Club, 2720 Pullman Road, Moscow Idaho 83843

This journal is a collection of lessons I have learned about how to learn about horses and contains only suggestions and my approach to learning about horses.

Patti's love for life and for all living creatures, human, equine, and all in between is evident in her stories. This collection will help even the most experienced horseperson.

Carrie Hrichak

The more you draw, the easier sketching becomes. Practice this sketch.

Add a background, landscape or color.

Use light strokes →

↑ Darken lines once
you know they work.

Sketch horses using pencil, charcoal,
conte, ink or paint.

Practice these horse sketches to learn how to draw horses.